96641745R00057

Made in the USA
Columbia, SC
30 May 2018